PRAISE FOR

Dave Moore

"Dave is very energetic and perfect for a group of professionals that need to laugh, connect, and listen to a fabulous storyteller. He is genuine and has lived through life changing events, which adds to his ability to capture the audience!"

Susan Griffith
New Story Educational System

"Dave was our construction company's keynote speaker for an annual week of training with a team-building theme. He was able to convey practical information as to how to build effective teams by developing communication skills, displaying a positive mental attitude, setting an example, etc. His messages were conveyed through his own interesting life experiences using humor and storytelling."

Kathy Hassett
CFO, Rampart-Hydro Services

"Dave's stories about courageous survival were told with humor and humility! And he had the entire audience engaged and laughing as the Association of Energy Service Companies annual summer meeting keynote speaker!"

Joyce Ryel
Association of Energy Service Companies

"Dave's stories really energized the crowd and his low-key personal style was just right for our staff appreciation event. He interacted well with the group and presented challenging situations in a light-hearted, yet instructional way. We have already recommended him for other events."

Jean Patterson
Director, DHCD Maryland

"Dave Moore was an excellent and dynamic speaker, who was very well received by everyone in the room. His stories are captivating, and he delivers a strong, positive message. He kept the room light and engaged. He has a great, magnetic personality, and people were truly inspired by his words and experiences. It was a pleasure working with Dave and his team to plan the event."

Caitlin Cole
Conference Program Manager
League of CA Cities

"Our group felt that Dave was real and genuine. Some speakers can come across as fake or superficial…not Dave."

Byron Bright
Progressive Executive

"We invited David to speak to our membership and he didn't disappoint. Dave is an enthusiastic speaker with a great presentation. The lessons taught through the experiences he shared were well received by our audience. Dave also took the time to stay after our event and answer questions from several of our members. If you are looking for an energetic speaker with a great message to share, David Moore is your man."

Jeff Ramsden
President
South Florida Business Aviation Association

Wake Up and Win

A THREE-TIME CRASH VICTIM'S JOURNEY
FROM SURVIVING TO THRIVING

DAVE MOORE

WAKE UP AND WIN

A THREE-TIME CRASH VICTIM'S JOURNEY FROM SURVIVING TO THRIVING

Copyright © 2020 by Dave Moore

To contact Dave:

Website	www.MooreMotivated.com
Contact Us	kendal@MooreMotivated.com
LinkedIn	https://www.linkedin.com/in/david-moore-3991192a/
Instagram:	https://www.instagram.com/Moore_Motivation/
Facebook	https://www.facebook.com/MooreMotivated/
Twitter	https://twitter.com/DMooreMotivated

To contact the publisher, Gravitas Press, visit https://GravitasPress.com.

Printed in the United States of America

ISBN 978-1-7322510-9-0

Book Strategist.....	Bonnie Budzowski
Cover Design	Bobbie Fox Fratangelo

Dedication

THIS BOOK IS DEDICATED to all individuals who want to remove the limitations imposed by society and its norms and step out to create the absolute best version of themselves.

Acknowledgments

*W*AKE UP AND WIN ISN'T ABOUT ME; it's about the journey I was led on by the Universe. Whatever name or acknowledgement you assign it, we share a connection, even as we make our own personal journeys. I am writing to share my journey, not to change yours.

This book is about taking all limits off your thinking—becoming childlike although not childish—so you can think big without self-imposed obstacles and achieve anything you want.

I acknowledge my mom, who has helped me take the risks I needed to grow by supporting me emotionally and financially. She never treated me as a baby but supported me, even when I floundered, on my path to reaching my goals. When situations were dire and I needed it, she lent me money that enabled me to make big moves or respond productively to the negative actions of others. I paid my mom back everything she ever lent me, and I hope I have given her much more than money in return.

My wife, Kendal, is amazing. Those who aspire to achieve great things in life need to be in a relationship with someone who believes they can do anything. Kendal's limitless love and support allow me to always strive for the best and achieve my definition of success, which extends far beyond financial wealth. My wife, who is so beautiful that she could be with anyone, chooses to be with me—when our journey is hard as well as when it is easy. I am beyond grateful for Kendal.

My love goes out to my first daughter, Addison, who was born into terrible family circumstances. My desire to be the best father possible to Addi was the impetus for my journey toward becoming the best I could be. Addi helped me start a journey to become a leader worth following as I want to be more to her than a financial provider. I want to model the skills Addi needs to be successful in fulfilling her purpose in life.

My younger children fill me with love and joy. Parenting them has been much easier, as they were born into a healthy marriage. My girls, Favianna, Olivia, and Julia continually motivate me to be the best me.

Many chickens and eagles have crossed my path in life. Their titles or status is not the determining factor in their identity as a chicken or eagle. I have had the good fortune to be groomed by some great business leaders. These eagles have given me insights and under-standing and have opened my mind to more than I can describe here.

I have an amazing connection with the Universe and have been given the opportunity to build this connection through struggle. I have been in poverty, on state insurance with a young wife, and the target of a wealthy family trying to keep my daughter away. I have felt whittled to the bone, fighting for what I knew was only fair and reasonable. I've also had times of victory and ease, now with a strong relationship with all of my kids and plenty of income. Because of the work I've done to find my true values and purpose in life, I know I can step out, even if it means leaving a lucrative job and moving in an unpopular direction. I thank the Universe for providing me this life of adventure.

Contents

PREFACE

WAKE UP AND WIN is my story of perseverance, overcoming obstacles, and being able to achieve or obtain everything I ever wanted.

This story begins with an account of my amazing survival from a dramatic plane crash. Even so, my life has not been charmed. In fact, my journey has been a roller coaster of triumphs, setbacks, and self-imposed obstacles. I have been battered, divorced, unemployed, underemployed, unappreciated, and bankrupt. I have often been my own worst enemy—even when what I wanted most was to be my best self. And, at times, I'm sure my actions have contributed to my being the villain in other's stories.

Against all odds, I have survived three plane crashes. I'm remarried to the best of all women, the love of my life; I've been gifted with wonderful children; and I've been in the top tier of earners in multiple companies.

I've been favored with amazing grace, mystery, and prosperity. I can't count the many hours I've spent reflecting on how it has all come together and the lessons I've learned. As founder of Moore Motivated and an international speaker, my mission is to share what I've discovered. It isn't all pretty, but it's important. It's all about waking up to become my best self and a leader worth following.

Our existence, from a biological standpoint, boils down to a series of wins and losses. Everyone loves to win. Football, poker, and performing in a play all have a greater appeal to us when we are successful and find praise for our abilities from our peers. It is in our DNA to want to succeed at what we do.

We have a constant need for purpose and drive, or a reason to wake up every morning and get out of bed. That drive comes in different forms, starting with our parents' care, growing into the drive to succeed in school and sports, and eventually to desiring healthy and meaningful relationships.

Many miss their best lives by accepting the definitions of success imposed from outside themselves and failing to figure out first what *they* want to do, or where their passions lie. I have heard many definitions about passion, long and drawn-out explanations. The core question for discovering your passion is simple: to what are you willing to dedicate your time, energy, and fullness of heart?

Your purpose and passion are unique to you—and your best contribution to the world needn't be at the top of a pyramid. Capable, intelligent, and able people work at NASA, and capable, intelligent, and able people stock the shelves at Walmart. If you know who you are and your work aligns with your purpose, you make the world a better place. When you achieve this alignment, you are a leader, regardless of your position. You are a role model that others wish to emulate and support. Money and support come your way because of the value you bring when who you are is aligned with what you do and offer the world.

Finding your purpose and passion isn't necessarily easy. Begin by summoning the courage to look deep inside; take each step that leads you to become the best person you can be. Trust that each step is part of a learning process that will ultimately lead you to your best self. Along the way, you will sometimes soar and sometimes seem stuck. It's a process full of mountains and valleys (or a roller coaster of triumphs and setbacks) as you learn and grow. If you are like me, some of your setbacks will be self-imposed. Your journey may be slow and arduous. It's okay.

At different points, we need to return to earlier lessons, some big and some small, when we move into a period of growth. A period of growth is simply a time when we face an obstacle larger than the others we have already overcome. As we struggle, the obstacle seems insurmountable, but it is merely an opportunity to break through our current comfort zone to achieve more than we ever have before.

My inspiration to share my story comes from a strong feeling of purpose and the belief that you will be able to relate to my experiences, that you'll find yourself in the triumphs and setbacks that have made up my journey so far. Along the way, I've learned that whatever milestones I've achieved or desire to achieve, I need to focus on what is before me. I need to focus on what the present situation requires of me, both in terms of what I can contribute and what I can learn. I don't get to move on until I learn the lesson at hand. Chances are, neither do you.

Welcome to my story. I hope it sheds some light on your own.

CHAPTER 1

A SWEET ASSIGNMENT GONE SOUR

I T WAS THE SWEETEST ASSIGNMENT I could imagine—until it nearly killed me.

As a 23-year-old student at Ohio University, I was struggling to pay my bills. For various reasons, I couldn't count on family for financial help. But I was determined to realize my dream of becoming a commercial airline pilot. Nothing was going to stop me from pursuing the career I'd been obsessed with since my childhood.

I had worked summers to get my pilot's and instructor's licenses, but I needed an aviation degree to get the job with American Airlines I had always wanted. Ironically, I was able to work as a flight instructor at the college on an as-needed basis, and I cobbled various other jobs together, including pumping plasma, to make ends meet. When I wasn't working, let's just say I enjoyed my booze and women.

I could hardly believe my luck when the university recommended me as a pilot and flight instructor to Dr. Michael, owner of two businesses and two high-performance airplanes, a Bellanca Super Viking and a Mooney TLS.

What a great part-time job it was to fly Dr. Michael and his family members between his company headquarters in Athens, Ohio, to his other company heaquarters in Steubenville, Ohio. I had access to awesome planes, and Dr. Michael, owner of a large real estate firm, even let me live in one of the company's basement apartments. The apartment had no heat, and I had to fill the toilet with a bucket of water to flush it, but given my financial state, I was more grateful than picky.

Dr. Michael was brilliant, but he was a lousy pilot. In fact, the doctor's son requested that I never actually allow Dr. Michael to become qualified to fly alone. I saw the wisdom in this request and agreed. Of course, I could still choose to give Dr. Michael flying lessons because I had access to the controls.

On December 17, 1997, exactly 94 years after the Wright brothers made their first flight at Kitty Hawk, Dr. Michael and I were having a routine lesson. We were doing high work—stalls and steep turns, working on maneuverability of the aircraft—when Dr. Michael insisted that I teach him to land. After all, his goal was to eventually fly himself back and forth between his two businesses. He reminded me that while flying is fun, it should also be practical.

We flew to Wheeling, West Virginia, to practice landing on a long, well-lit runway. Everything was going well until Dr. Michael insisted we practice on the runway in Steubenville. I didn't like to use this runway, even when I was doing the landing. It is short and narrow, sitting on the edge of a steep, wooded hill. This runway requires extra precision and leaves no room for any error.

But Dr. Michael was paying me 10 bucks an hour, so off we flew to Steubenville. With no control tower and no other planes around at the small airport, we were able to take off and land as many times as we wanted without concern for other aircraft—or even filing a flight plan.

As we took off and landed multiple times, I did my job as instructor with gritted teeth. After one shaky landing, Dr. Michael remarked, "I scare the crap out of you, don't I?"

The wind was calm as we took off for our final practice landing. We raced down the runway with Dr. Michael in control. Our nose was just off the runway when we heard a loud boom—and the airplane snapped 90 degrees to the right. Although we didn't know it, we had collided with a deer.

With the plane crippled and heading toward the refueling area, I grabbed the controls. The right wing was down, limp, while the left wing was in the air. I kept trying to upright the aircraft, but it just wouldn't turn. In desperation, I stomped on the rudder and let myself breathe again as this got us around the refueling area and a certain fiery death. At least we wouldn't cause a catastrophic explosion.

Now the airplane was headed for the hangar, and I struggled with the controls, trying to crash on the runway and spare any lives or property on the ground. The next thing I knew, branches of trees were racing toward us. As the treetops became menacing, I said, "Dr. Michael, this is it."

We crashed into a huge tree . . . and the world went black.

When I came to, I was at the bottom of the airplane, suspended in my harness. Dr. Michael's full weight was on top of me, and I was suffocating. My face had literally ripped off in the crash, and both my nose ports and mouth were clogged with mud. My right hand was wedged beneath the front of the airplane, and I couldn't move it. Using my left hand to rip out the mud so that I could breathe, I registered the obvious: we had crashed. Then I had a thought in keeping with my arrogance at the time, "This is a dream. This stuff doesn't happen to Dave Moore."

Dream or no dream, I reached for the microphone to call for help. It was dead.

I didn't own a cell phone, and for some reason, the plane's Emergency Locator Transmitter (ELT), designed to transmit a distress signal in the event of an accident, failed.

My adrenaline kicked in and I knew we had to get away from the plane's fuel tank. I started screaming, "Dr. Michael, get off me!" No response. Assuming he was dead, I started a panicky struggle to free myself from him and the plane. Shoulders pinned, I fought to pull out my trapped hand from the front of the plane with the power of my legs. The hand finally came free, leaving my fingernails and a lot of skin behind.

I unfastened myself from my harness and got out from under Dr. Michael, still thinking he was dead. Then I noticed his eyelids flicker. I dragged him away from the plane and along with me to get help.

About an hour later, Dr. Michael came to. In his shock, he said, "David, David, you forgot my shoe!" The doctor was missing the classic leather penny loafer he wore, complete with the penny. There we were, in the middle of nowhere, with no way to signal for help, and I found myself thinking about Dr. Michael's shoes. I wondered where the idea to put a penny in a shoe came from. Oddly, this would be one of the clearest moments in my life.

Before long, Dr. Michael said, "David, we aren't both going to make it. You are young—go get yourself help."

Still full of adrenaline, I responded, "Nobody is going to die out here."

* * * * *

The crash took place around 7 p.m. I dragged myself and Dr. Michael through the woods toward the hangar until 9 p.m. Once my initial surge of adrenaline began to lag, every joint, muscle, and bone in my body screamed in pain. Even so, I knew that if I stopped moving, we would die. Dragging a full-grown man through the woods during an Ohio December wasn't easy. I remember crawling through water, and then seeing a hill in front of me. I said, "God, you're going to make me climb this hill. This is ridiculous."

Finally, we reached the top, and I could see a light on in the hangar, about half a mile away. After two hours of dragging myself and Dr. Michael, I couldn't move another inch. I screamed frantically until a guy who was working at the hangar came out with a big flashlight. His first words, seeing us sprawled just out of the woods, were, "Car or plane?"

After calling 911, the guy attended first to Dr. Michael, who was close to death. He put me on the running board of a fire engine. I asked for a cigarette. He said, "I don't think you need a cigarette right now." I asked him to pull me up so that I could see the mirror on the truck. He said, "I don't think you need a mirror. You just need to sit there."

The emergency responders took Dr. Michael in a Life Flight helicopter to Pittsburgh. They loaded me in an ambulance and headed for Trinity Medical Center in Steubenville.

My experience in the emergency room was surreal. In shock, with eyes swelled shut, I saw lights and people moving, but I didn't really know what was going on. Police were a vague presence asking if there were more people on the plane. Lacking a flight plan or an accident site, emergency personnel had no way of knowing if other passengers were wounded, stranded in the woods.

A nurse named Tracy stayed with me all night, alternately holding my hand or foot. I was anxious about whether I was going to live or die. True to myself at the time, however, I noticed that Tracy sounded hot. The idea of connecting with a hot chick faded into humiliation when the medical team cut off my pants. I was wearing Winnie the Pooh boxers. "Aw," said Tracy, "my Pooh bear." I gave up caring about anything.

I remember my mom arriving and I also remember refusing to allow the emergency room doctor to stitch my face. I allowed him to stitch my hand, and then I just wanted to go home. Ignoring my request, the hospital staff called in an emerging plastic surgeon who was pioneering a new technique. This doctor was appalled at the sloppy way the emergency room doctor had stitched my hand.

Once I was stabilized, the press, the Federal Aviation Administration (FAA), and the National Transportation Safety Board (NTSB) all wanted to talk to me. The press was hailing me as a hero for saving Dr. Michael, but hero was an identity I could not embrace. In fact, the main reason I struggled to stay alive the day of the crash was that, faced with death, I was profoundly ashamed of the person I was or fell short of being. My lifestyle was selfish and devoid of meaning and purpose. I had begged God to allow me to survive the crash so that I could become the person I was meant to be. I just couldn't die without a chance to get my life right.

I was nervous about the FAA and NTSB investigations, sure that I was in big trouble. Surprisingly, the investigators weren't aggressive or accusing. The lead investigator explained that the first responders had begun looking for the crash site and other victims in the deep woods at 9 p.m.—about the same time Dr. Michael and I were being rushed to our respective hospitals. The next day, officials put a plane in the air and finally found the site.

The investigator said to me, "Son, I've investigated a lot of accidents. I don't know if you believe in God or not, but there's no reason you should be alive right now. For one thing, when you crashed, the plane separated, and you and your passenger were dragged 160 feet away from the ignition source. That's how your face got ripped up. What's more, I followed the path you made from the crash site back to the hangar. There is no mathematical way that you could have cleared the ravine. I need to know how you found your way out of those woods."

I explained, "I looked up in the sky and saw a light. I followed the light."

Eyes wide, the investigator leaned in and was silent.

"I saw the rotating beacon, and I followed it."

Amazed, the investigator said, "There's no logical reason that you are alive."

AFTERMATH

D URING ONE OF MY SURGERIES, the hospital staff removed the mirrors from my room. The doctors were concerned that the sight of my own mangled face would send me into shock. While that prevented me from seeing the worst of my injuries, it didn't prevent me from knowing that I had just narrowly escaped death. The days after experiencing this event were surreal.

Outside my hospital window was a gazebo where doctors, nurses, and other staff members congregated to smoke. Lying in my bed, just a few days after the surgery, I could hear the group talking about the petty details of their lives, such as what they were having for lunch, which celebrities were vacationing in exotic places, and what plans they had for the weekend. Lying in my mirrorless room, with my various body parts stitched together and covered with bandages, I was stunned.

Merely three days before, I had been a hair's breadth away from death, and these people were conversing about trivial things. It just blew me away. At 23 years old, with the naiveté of youth and a puffed-out chest from my piloting accomplishments, I had assumed the world revolved around me, as most of us do. Suddenly, I understood that I was a hiccup on the face of the earth. What a wake-up call.

This reality, and the fresh knowledge of both the fragility of life and my body, completely changed my perspective. I had mistakenly thought that since I was young and strong, I was also invincible, with countless tomorrows to live an admirable life. To say I was shaken, as well as physically shattered, is an understatement. But I was alive.

During the seemingly eternal struggle to get myself and Dr. Michael out of the woods after the crash, I had begged God to save me. I didn't beg for my life because I was young and still thought I had a worthy and long life to live. I don't even remember being afraid. I only remember that I was too embarrassed to die. I saw with great clarity that I had been wasting my life in purposeless pursuits. How could I end my life in such an unworthy state?

I believed God had saved me from the crash, and the opinion of the investigator who saw no reason I should be alive bolstered that belief. During my time in the hospital, I was profoundly humbled. I was stunned and ashamed of the person I had become. At the same time, I was determined to change into someone that would

Chapter 2

make God proud. Today, I think of it as becoming a leader worth following. On that day in the hospital, I just knew I had to become my best self. My commitment was solid, but I had no idea of the process I would need to go through to get there.

The dramatic crash, the missing crash site, and the circumstances of my and Dr. Michael's survival had been news over several days, and members of the press wanted to hear from me. I remember passing through a receiving line, feeling overwhelmed by the noise. People were shouting, "Dave Moore's a hero." I wanted to cover my head in my hands and escape.

One man was in stark contrast to the crowd. Although he was in a wheelchair, this man exuded strength, with strong features and a commanding voice. He said to me, "*You* carried him out, didn't you?"

"No. No. No," I answered, even more shaken.

I knew I didn't deserve credit, that I wasn't a hero. Yet, I couldn't explain how Dr. Michael made it out from the crash site. Given what I had been told by investigators, I couldn't explain how I made it out either. It's a mystery that I can't explain even today. Looking back, I can't even be sure the man in the wheelchair was real. Either way, the encounter was so strong and clear that I can see his face and hear his voice even now.

Many experiences surrounding the accident were surreal. Facts, circumstances, and feelings all converged in mysterious ways, such that I was confident God had his hand on my life. Somehow, I had survived a near fatal crash. The plane had broken in two, with my half skidding for many yards. That's how the skin of my face got scraped off—and how Dr. Michael and I eventually stopped some distance from the gas tank, saving us from a fiery death. I clearly remember talking to God, but I had hit my head pretty hard.

Although I had multiple injuries, and my face had literally been ripped off, the paramedics had taken me to a small Steubenville hospital rather than a major trauma center. The reconstructive surgery on my face was performed by a pioneer of a leading-edge technique, who happened to be in Steubenville at the time. Now I have scars on my hands—but not on my face. In fact, I look better than I did before the accident. When I was being discharged from the hospital, the surgeon referred to my face as his Sistine Chapel.

The crash itself was determined to be caused by a deer striking the plane and categorized as an act of God. No charges were filed against me, and no marks from the crash mar my record as a pilot.

As amazing as all these circumstances were, they weren't easy to digest. The months following the accident were filled with pain and internal struggle. The love of a puppy, Bailey, became a profound comfort.

My girlfriend at the time and I had recently gotten Bailey, flea-bitten and full of worms, from the pound. We took Bailey to the vet, who said, "I appreciate what you are trying to do for this puppy, but I give him a 50/50 chance to live." Bailey recovered and went from being barely able to walk to a bundle of energy with a zest for living. Upon my release from the hospital, they brought her to stay with me at my mom's where I was recovering.

Those close to me kept urging me to get out of the house and back into the world, but I was reluctant. My head was swollen, and I knew I looked ugly. One day, I agreed to go to the mall, just to get out. I was standing in the food court when I heard the fear in a little girl's voice as she screamed to her father, "Daddy, what's wrong with that man's face?!" After that, Bailey became my therapeutic and beloved companion.

For as long as I could remember, I had been enthralled with airplanes. Aviation had been my solid foundation as well as my soaring thrill. All my visions of the future had me in a cockpit wearing an American Airlines uniform. I had been the guy who was quick to remind others that airplanes were safer than cars.

All that had changed in an instant. Suddenly, not only was my trust in the safety of flying lost, but my understanding of life itself had flipped. I knew without a doubt there was more to life than airplanes—more than anything we see. And the near-death experience had left me crippled with anxiety.

I left the hospital as soon as I possibly could, and I got off the pain pills quickly as well. Dr. Michael had given me some anti-anxiety medicine (and kept this fact off my medical records), but I didn't like how the medication made me feel, so I got off that too.

Roughly 45 days after the accident, I was back at the university and flying again—because that's what I knew, and I didn't want to think about anything else. It was just too much to process. I was different at my core, but I didn't know how to live differently. Flying was second nature to me, something I was good at. Even as I had come to realize that I had a higher life purpose than flying airplanes, I struggled to get back to my normal. From a practical standpoint, it's all I knew.

Of course, I was no longer anywhere near my old normal. I was dissatisfied with the person I had been. I knew I had natural charisma and talent, and that I had used those gifts selfishly rather than for the good of others. I was afraid to die until I had become the person I was meant to be, my best self. And I felt death was chasing me.

To say I was an anxious mess is an understatement. I had multiple panic attacks every day, and although the doctors explained the physiology of these attacks, I was often convinced I was suffering a heart attack. I simply couldn't calm myself down.

While a healthy heart rate is between 60 and 80 beats per minute, my rate hovered around 120 beats per minute at rest. Walking down the street one day, I prayed that God would just take me because I felt I couldn't live that way another day. Ready to die or not, I just wanted the anxiety to end.

When it came to flying, my confidence and bravado had turned into abject fear—a fear I obviously had to hide from others. During a flight, I would torture myself with "what-if" scenarios, forcing myself to identify how I would handle any number of unlikely events. This made me a good pilot, but I was perpetually on edge.

I remember one flight on which I was piloting a F33 Bonanza owned by Ohio University. I had dropped off a passenger and was alone on the return flight. I had such a severe panic attack that I put the plane on autopilot and hoped it would run out of gas and gently land in an unpopulated area.

Somehow, for the next four or five months, I kept flying and working as a staff instructor at the university. I got stuck in a vicious cycle: I couldn't sleep at night, so I drank to put myself to sleep. I built a resistance to the alcohol, so I needed to drink even more to sleep. The next day, my mind would be unclear. And the cycle just continued.

After a bad weather experience flying Dr. Michael's other airplane, the Mooney TLS, from Las Vegas to Ohio in bad weather, I finally admitted to myself that I had to stop flying. I can't begin to explain the sense of loss that came with that decision. Suddenly, I had no focus, no path forward, and no job.

I went back to work at the pizza shop in my Pennsylvania hometown, where I'd worked during high school, and tried to sort out the meaning of life. I later got a job in sales and spent a couple of years doing well financially in that field. I was determined to figure my life out, but the path forward was anything but clear. I did lots of thinking during that confusing and humbling time. Looking back, I realize that I needed to be stripped of pride and pretense before I could rebuild. I've had to revisit this lesson at various points on my journey. Each time I got too big for myself, I got knocked back. Growth is a process in which pride and self-sufficiency are obstructions. And tomorrow is never guaranteed.

* * * * *

One day, I looked up to the sky as an airplane flew by. In a moment of clarity, I asked myself, "What are you doing down here?"

I applied for a job at the Beaver County Airport in Western Pennsylvania as a flight instructor. Before I could take the job, however, I needed to become recertified. In the process, I wrecked the simulator, further humbling myself. After all the skill I had amassed as a pilot, I felt like an incompetent novice. But I got the job and soon began to excel again.

The next steps in my career are shrouded in the kind of mystery that also shrouded my accident. Early in 2011, for unclear reasons, I decided to apply to the Coast Guard. I had never wanted to be in the Coast Guard, as it was a tough path, involving 17 weeks of hard training. Once the training is completed, there's no guarantee you'll fly. You might end up on a ship. Even so, I found myself walking into a recruiting office.

The recruiting officer took one look at me and succinctly declared, "You're too fat."

Three months later, I returned to that same office, a much slimmer version of myself. The recruiting officer remembered me and, impressed with my self-discipline, said he would help me apply for Officer Candidate School. He warned me that my chances were slim, given that the Coast Guard usually promotes from within. He told me that the only reason he would do the hard work to put my officer package forward was because I had made such an effort. The officer told me to expect to hear from the Coast Guard by July of that year. July came and went, with no call.

Meanwhile, the commercial airlines were hiring. I had the chance to secure my dream job. Neither I nor my peers understood why I wasn't jumping at the chance. After all, if I took a position in the Coast Guard, I'd lose eight to ten years of seniority if I later took a job with a commercial airline. Still, I hesitated.

In August, my dad called to ask me if I had applied to the Coast Guard. The Guard had lost my phone number and finally tracked me down through my dad, David J. Moore. My application, which identified me as David J. Moore Jr., had been selected. The Coast Guard had simply gone through the phone book to find me. The message was that I needed to call to give my decision to accept or reject the job right away.

Given that the Coast Guard wouldn't guarantee a flight position, I didn't know what to do. In a quandary, I spent the evening drinking with a flight attendant I was dating. Later that night, still somewhat inebriated and always dramatic, I prayed for a sign telling me what to do. I turned on the television and began watching a preacher, something I'd never done before.

The preacher began to tell a well-worn story about a man who lived by a river. The man hears a radio announcement informing residents by the river to leave because of unsafe conditions. The man doesn't hurry to leave because he is a religious man, confident that God will save him.

In most versions of this story, God sends a rowboat to rescue the man. The man waves the boat away, saying, "God will save me." Next, God sends a helicopter, and the man makes the same response. Finally, the man drowns. When he gets to heaven, the man asks God why he didn't save him. God says, "I sent a radio announcement, a rowboat, and a helicopter to save you, but you wouldn't listen!"

In the television preacher's version, God sent a Coast Guard boat. The reference to the Coast Guard surprised me, but I decided it was a coincidence.

"Next," the preacher said, "God sent a Coast Guard helicopter ..."

I swore in the next day, on a hot August morning.

A month later, terrorist planes struck the World Trade Center. As one of many consequences, commercial airlines laid off hordes of pilots. I was in the Coast Guard, which turned out to be the perfect career position at the time.

CHAPTER 3

BEFORE YOU FLY,
YOU GOTTA FLOAT

LIKE EVERY OTHER AMERICAN CITIZEN, I was pro-foundly affected by the events of 9/11. I remember making a trip to Walmart just after the attacks. At the door, I encountered a woman who seemed to be in her 60s, providing "security" at the entrance. She was weeping.

It was a bizarre image, one that embodies the shock, lack of preparedness, grief, and determination of the country at that time. The store was sold out of American flags, but I was able to find a few remaining patriotic CDs. I purchased one.

In the face of the terrorist attacks, I was especially proud to go to the Coast Guard's Officer Candidate School. My desire to save lives was genuine, but my expectations of the life I was entering were complete fantasy. Not a military man, I was headed to 17 long weeks of some of the toughest training on the planet. I blasted my patriotic CD in my car the entire drive there.

The recruiting officer in the suburbs of Pittsburgh didn't prepare me for the challenges I would face at school in New London, Connecticut, that October 2001. When I asked him what to expect in Officer Candidate School, the recruiter asked if I knew how to fold my socks and underwear. He said, "If you can do that, you'll do fine at school."

I'm told that the only officer candidate training program more rigorous than the Coast Guard's is the Marine's. I soon found myself running across a field with a M1 Garand rifle over my head, wondering what on earth I was doing. Ready to quit in a heartbeat, I discovered that I wasn't allowed to make that decision until two weeks into the training. I had signed myself in, and I was stuck.

Once the two weeks were completed, I called my mom to let her know I was quitting and would be coming home. But Mom managed to speak first, telling me how proud my family members were of my service to the country. By the time it was my turn to talk, I was too embarrassed to quit.

While I made it through Officer Candidate School, I never did adopt a military attitude. I was always in trouble for being mouthy and sharp-tongued. My superiors did not appreciate my quick wit and funny comments. One of my instructors declared that he would keep me on PT (discipline via physical training) until the day I died.

Fortunately, I was in good shape when I arrived at Officer Candidate School, but I had more than the physical demands involved to worry about. We all knew that the chances of being assigned to flight school were slim. In fact, we knew that out of our class of 60-plus candidates, only three would move on to flight school. Others would end up on a boat. As for me, I not only didn't like the water, I wasn't even a good swimmer. All I ever wanted to do was fly.

As our time at the school came to an end, I was more than a little nervous. Thankfully, I earned the highest score in the class on the Aviation Aptitude Test. My score on military bearing, on the other hand, was average at best. Would it be enough?

I remember Billet Night, when everybody gets together to receive assignments that will last for several years and influence their entire careers. Dreams are fulfilled and crushed on Billet Night. I stood listening to the announcement of which candidates were being assigned to flight school. The announcements came in alphabetical order—and the third name began with "L," one alphabet step before my "M" for Moore.

I stood stunned, my upcoming years of commitment to the Guard running through my mind. One of my instructors, who knew how badly I wanted to fly, mocked me. "Get used to wearing that duty belt,

Moore," he said. "You are headed to an icebreaker in the Bering Sea."

And then came another announcement, which the instructor knew was coming. Because our class had so many good candidates, our superiors had taken a flight spot from another class. That spot was awarded to me, and I began primary and intermediate flight training in Pensacola, Florida in May of 2002.

I was all set with the academics and the flight training. I had a real problem, however, with my fear and discomfort in water.

Naturally, anyone desiring to earn their wings from Navy Flight School must pass a rigorous water survival class. I kept up with the class in water survival all the way to the "tread and float" portion of our training. To pass this test, you had to tread water with a flight suit, boots, and a weighted vest on. You had to tread water for so long, then you had to be able to float forward— not on your back, and slow your heart rate. At this point, I hit a barrier. I was terrified.

Each time I tried the tread and float, I digressed, losing more confidence in myself and my ability to complete the drill. How could I get progressively worse with extra training? Simple, the problem was in my head.

We started practicing for the tread and float with our flight suits on. Then we added weighted vests. I was able to complete both of those evolutions. Adding boots to the picture gave me the greatest difficulty, but I was still able to pass.

The instructor explained that adding a helmet would make us more buoyant, but that some people would have a tougher time completing the exercise because of the sense of confinement you feel in the helmet. I thought that was the dumbest thing I had ever heard. I was pumped that we were getting a buoyant helmet, meaning that water survival training was almost complete for me. I just needed to complete the final evolution of the tread and float and somehow muster up a mile swim in a flight suit.

Once I passed water survival, I would be good to graduate Navy Flight School.

On my first attempt wearing the helmet, I ended up at the bottom of the pool. I was shattered, as my confidence had been building through the different evolutions of water survival.

Growing up, I always thought I was a competent swimmer, but I was outside of my comfort zone, and competing against high achievers from various parts of the world.

There I was full of fresh moxie from completing Officer Candidate School (OCS), 17 weeks of the most ridiculous hell I could imagine. OCS had provided the opportunity to build my strength as a person, both mentally and physically, to believe I could work past any obstacle. How was it that I couldn't complete this tread and float test?

Eventually, I was able to trace my struggle and fear in this situation to a childhood experience. As a teenager, I was on a hike with a church group when we came up to a waterfall. I got swept up in the moment with some of the guys, and we dared each other to see who could climb the highest and jump.

We one-upped each other until my third or so jump went awry. The falls had eroded the earth, so the rock gradually sloped back as you went higher up the falls. To avoid a disaster, you needed to get a running start and jump out and toward the side of the fall, avoiding both the rocks and the churning whitewash created directly below the falls.

On my last jump, I slipped while trying to leap out and away from the rocks. My heart pounded as I was falling, anticipating being crushed on the rocks below. I can't remember what went through my head, but I do remember that I was 100 percent convinced I was going to hit the rocks. I didn't know if I would die or just be busted up badly.

Fortunately, I missed the rocks and ended up in the water, tumbling into the white-water wash from the falls. Around and around, it was like being in a washing machine and not knowing which way was up. I was under the water about as long as I could have survived.

Finally, my arm latched around a dead tree that had fallen lying against the falls. I was able to climb up and out of the water. I shifted from having a big ego to a shattered reality—in a single jump.

After this experience, I wasn't afraid of the water, but I was afraid of drowning. Passing the tread and float was never about my physical ability to swim; it was about overcoming my fear, the feeling I remembered from tumbling in that water and feeling the horrific edge of what it would be like to drown.

That helmet did, in fact, give me a sense of confinement and terror. I tried and failed to complete the tread and float several times. My anxiety tightened my muscles, causing me to sink in the pool and hyperventilate. I had to be pulled out with a rescue ring or by a rescue swimmer, and I became increasingly demoralized each time.

I got rolled back several classes and sent to remedial swim. I began to think that I would return to my hometown as the guy who made it through 17 weeks of Coast Guard OCS and 17 weeks of learning discipline—having become an aviator who breathed, slept, and used aviation as a focal point in life—only to return home as a failure because he was afraid to swim.

How did I turn this situation around and pass that test? I finally took my mental stand. I thought about what I had to lose. I could not bear the thought of not being allowed to punch holes in the sky in that T-34. Loops, rolls, formation flying, and the beginning of one of the most rewarding careers of my life sat just on the other side of a simple tread and float evolution.

I decided to make a last attempt at passing the tread and float. I would be coming out of the pool one of two ways: successfully or in a body bag.

I refocused, not on the task in front of me, but on fond memories of Christmas Eve with great family and friends, imagining how it would feel that year to show up as a member of the Coast Guard.

During the float portion of the test, I envisioned my dog, Bailey, gliding though the water, swimming after ducks at the local park. I allowed myself to feel the enjoyment she got from swimming.

Once I refocused, I was no longer at the "end of my rope," or struggling to manage the minimum time to stay in the water to complete the test. Connecting with my passion for aviation had enabled me to shift perspective and put enough time, effort, and energy into finding the solution to the problem. I knew I was physically in shape to complete the task at hand. The problem was with my mind and preconceived outcomes. I was allowing one negative experience to paralyze me and block me from achieving an important goal. I was letting fear control me.

In graduating from Navy Flight School, I not only overcame my fear of drowning, but also overcame a doubt that might have crippled me for the rest of my days. Since the crash, so much had changed in my mind. I had harbored a fear that I was mentally handicapped, and no one would tell me. I was afraid my mental aptitude was less than it had been, and others were pitying me. Having pushed forward, I now knew this wasn't true.

Momentum is a powerful thing. Once you start to win, beat your obstacles, or achieve your goals, it gets easier and easier to face your fears, stretch yourself, and win again. Failures and setbacks can shake you up, but they don't need to define you. If you read the life stories of millionaires, you'll discover that many experience failures and even bankruptcy, only to come right back for the big win. They focus on the future and the disciplines that led them to wealth in the first place. The stories of great Olympian athletes reveal the same lessons.

Success in life comes from the freedom to pursue the goals that are most important to you. To win, you need to be free from fear, the need for approval, greed, or any obstacle that holds you back from being your best self. Not everyone needs to like you, appreciate you, or be at the same point in life as you are.

The only person that needs to like you or approve of you is you. This is a truth I had to wake up to, and, as you will see, it didn't come easily. One big step was getting off autopilot and identifying and facing the roots of my fears. I finally passed my water survival test and moved on to my next growth experience.

.

CHAPTER 4

BIG ACCOMPLISHMENTS, BIG MISTAKE

UPON GRADUATING from advanced flight training, I was given my choice of assignments. I chose to go to Air Station Miami as a HU-25 Falcon pilot. I brought Christi, a girl I had met at Hooters in Mobile, Alabama, to live with me.

My relationship with Christi broke up after two years, but I stayed in Miami, rising through the ranks, for a five-year period. During those years, I got to have some of the greatest experiences doing things I never thought I would do. Every day seemed to have a new and exciting operation to complete, and each of those operations taught me lessons you don't get in a typical job.

In one assignment, I was on a crew of five that was called up to Guantanamo Bay, Cuba, to pick up 10 kilos of uncut cocaine following a major Coast Guard drug bust. We were to return the cocaine to the capital city of

Tegucigalpa in Honduras, where the government allegedly planned to prosecute the dealers.

Walking into the hangar to get the cocaine, we heard a firm voice saying, "Sirs, please stop." It turns out we had gone to the wrong hangar, where we encountered a van full of al-Qaeda. Looking into the eyes of those men, I saw anger and hatred like I had never seen before. I still shiver to think of it.

Once we got safely to the right hangar and picked up our load, we flew the Falcon Jet to Honduras. I was at the controls, flying to a third world airport, outdated, and with a dangerous approach. When we broke out of the clouds, I couldn't see the airport because it was below us in a deep valley. The only way to get there was to circle down the mountain, with the airbrakes out, to get to the low-lying runway.

Focusing intently and beginning to circle down to the right, I heard a crew member say, "High five to Jesus!" He was goofing off about a statue on the mountain while I was white-knuckled and trying to get us safely on the ground. Heading down the mountain, I couldn't see where I was going, until suddenly the runway was right beneath the plane's nose. We landed safely, but not without tense moments.

The crew stepped out of the plane, expecting to be met by the Drug Enforcement Agency (DEA) for protection. But something had gone wrong, and the DEA was late.

There we were, five unarmed young men, in an extremely uncomfortable position. A man in a decorated uniform came forward. Based on his bearing and the people surrounding him, this man was clearly an important figure, well-supported and guarded. Soldier kids, maybe 14 years old, stood in their jeeps, brandishing machine guns. The smell in the air was decidedly hostile. José, a crew member we were relying on to translate, said, "I can't understand the dialect."

In the silence that followed, I tried to read the situation. I felt certain that any world leader of this man's status would speak English. We shouldn't need a translator. This man, who we later found out was the president's brother, was deliberately intimidating us.

I asked myself what the man wanted, and I guessed it was respect from what he perceived as arrogant Americans. Testing my theory, I stepped back, took a sweeping look around, and directed my words to José, "Tell him he has a beautiful country." The atmosphere changed instantly, and the president's brother ended up putting his arm around me and giving us a tour. On the flight home, my buddies joked that I had gotten along so well with the dignitary that I'd be the next president of Honduras.

This is an example of the amazing opportunities and responsibilities that come with the military. It also depicts one of my early lessons about effective communication. When we avoid a quick reaction and step back to understand what the other person wants and needs, we increase our chances of a positive outcome exponentially.

During my time in the Coast Guard, I flew through three hurricanes. The first one occurred early in my career when the air station alarm went off to launch the Falcon Jet for a rescue. The winds and rain were so strong that I thought the alarm was signaling a test. Not so—a man was stranded with his cat on a yacht off the coast of Miami. When we radioed for permission to use the airways, the response was, "You are cleared to go wherever you need to go. No one else is out here."

An engineering commander with a strong personality was at the controls. We were all nervous as we flew in and out of the hurricane. Winds well over 100 mph pummeled us as we flew low over a turbulent sea.

I was reading the aviation map as we flew through heavy clouds. The pilot was steering to the left with the intention of hugging the intercoastal landmass. I could see on the map that if we continued this course, we would hit a tower. When I told the commander this, he pushed back. I found myself as a young officer summoning up the courage needed to stand up to the commander. Our lives were at stake. Thankfully, the man, the cat, and the crew made it safely back to shore.

In the second instance, I was flying with the same commander doing a pre-hurricane assessment off the NASA space coast. We were filming the coast so that we could assess the damage after the hurricane. A marine safety officer was with us.

We were 50 feet into restricted air space when an emergency locator transmitter started going off. We had to land in Daytona to get more fuel before we headed out for the rescue. Looking for an adventure, the marine safety officer, not essential to the mission, wanted to come along.

He hadn't bargained for the fact that we would need to fly into the hurricane. We flew 100 feet off the water above a turbulent, emerald-green sea until we located an abandoned boat that had gotten sucked into the storm.

On our way back to shore, we punched through the eye of the hurricane into an eerie calm. Then we were back in it again.

While all this was going on, the marine safety officer was repeatedly retching. When we finally got off the plane, he was green around the gills and covered in vomit. I couldn't help but ask, "Hey, would you like a group hug?"

My third hurricane was off the coast of Corpus Christi, Texas. Hurricane Ike had knocked out the power, and the Army, Air Force, and Coast Guard were all headed to downtown Houston. Although I was a seasoned Falcon pilot at this point, I remember this as some of the most intense flying I'd ever done. I was named on-scene commander to coordinate with the different agencies on the scene. I remember thinking, "I'm just a guy from a small town outside of Pittsburgh. Don't we have someone more qualified for this job?" That's the way it is in the military: you are called to big responsibilities when lives are at stake.

A final example of a great opportunity that came during my time with the military was closer to home and much more fun. Alex, a young guy I was mentoring, happened to share my alma mater of Ohio University. Alex got permission from an aircraft commander, who was also an Ohio University alumnus, for the two of us to do a flyby in the Falcon Jet for the University's homecoming one year.

The Coast Guard made this a recruiting event, and Alex and I were interviewed in our flight suits. The whole thing was an incredible thrill. Where else but the military would you get an opportunity like this?

* * * * *

My first assignments as a leader were in Miami, leading a group in charge of security and communication codes. I got burned and learned some valuable lessons. It was important to me to be nice, to be well-liked. After a difficult experience in which a subordinate walked all over me, my commanding officer remarked, "Dave, being nice isn't nice for anyone." I learned the disappointing lesson: given the chance to do the right thing, not everyone will take it.

I had a friend whose family lived in a small town in Pennsylvania, many miles away from Miami. He told me about his sister who was a doctor. Based on what my friend described, I became enchanted with his family. At one point, my friend said, "Do you want my beautiful sister's phone number?"

I called his sister, Krista, and began to get to know her, hoping that she and her family might be the ticket to the future I wanted for myself. My father had left my mother and our family when I was a young adult, caus-ing deep pain and longstanding practical life problems. I was determined to have a different family experience. I wanted to be the quintessential husband and dad.

I didn't realize that I was looking for someone to fill the broken places within myself. Even in the best of cir-cumstances, this doesn't work. In this case, I soon learned that the description my friend had given of Krista and the family was a series of lies. For example, Krista was a nurse, not a doctor. For some reason, I ig-nored this and other red flags and got deeply involved.

I would prefer to keep Krista and her family com-pletely out of this book, but that would leave too big of a gap. The result of my marriage to Krista is a spectacular child, Addison, who has changed me for the better. And the experience of the marriage dictated the next 11 years of my life and continues to be an influence. The trauma of that marriage and my commitment to be the best fa-ther to my child forced me to grow into the man I am to-day. These things drove me to discover and practice the principles I describe in this book. I found my way as a result of struggle, hard knocks, and a persistent love for my daughter.

Krista, a small-town nurse, had never been with an-other guy and had never lived away from her Western Pennsylvania family home. Even so, she got a job in Miami and came to live there. When we married in

2007, I already knew that the marriage wasn't viable, that I was in love with Krista's fictitious family rather than Krista herself. Grasping for the good life, I went forward anyway. How I reconciled the vow I had made never to divorce with this decision is a mystery. It shines a light on what I believed about myself at the time—that I was broken and unworthy of a better life partner.

From the start, my relationship to Krista was a nightmare, but once in the marriage, I gave it my all. I tried everything in my power to make my wife happy. It turns out that Krista was a bully, and an anxious one at that. And she hated Miami because it felt too big, too overwhelming to her.

In her unhappiness, Krista constantly put me down. My head was always spinning, and I drank. From Miami, I accepted a transfer back to Corpus Christi, Texas, where I was promoted to supply officer, in charge of $90 million dollars and 30+ people. Krista and I thought the move would be good for our marriage—because Corpus Christi was small compared to Miami. Hopefully, Krista would feel more at ease there.

I didn't really want the promotion that went with the move, especially in supply. I wanted to be in operations where I could fly my airplane! All I ever wanted to do was fly.

I didn't know anything about supply, and I never learned. I succeeded in the job by focusing on the people. For example, a supply worker was going to lose his job because excess body weight was causing him to fail the fitness test. I decided to meet with him before work each day. In doing so, I discovered two important facts: First, this guy was studying to be a CPA, and he had skills we could certainly use in supply. Second, he was a natural-born runner. We worked together and saved his job.

Another employee confided in me about his family's challenges in raising a special needs child. He asked to come into work a half hour late each day in order to drop his kid off at school. In return, he offered to stay an additional extra hour after work. My superior officer was against making any adjustment, saying, "We're the Coast Guard." I still managed to make things work for this family.

Because of situations like these, my people worked their tails off for me. In fact, we won an award for best supply shop in the entire Coast Guard. And, in two years on the job, I was promoted up the ranks. I became an instructor pilot, then stand evaluation officer, and finally chairman of the Flight Evaluation Board.

While my career was soaring in Corpus Christi, I was a mess inside. Krista was no happier than she had been in Miami, and she constantly blamed me, calling me an alcoholic and even a pussy. Krista had quit her job as a nurse as soon as we were married. She suffered from social anxiety and chose not to participate in the many things the military offered to keep family members engaged. Her only close connections were her parents, who were far away.

As a result, Krista spent her days alone with three dogs. It seemed she spent the time thinking about what was wrong with me. Sometimes I felt like I was coming home to Judge Judy. At other times, I felt like I was living with a 12-year-old. Krista had tantrums and lacked any sense of accountability. She wanted everything, including a new career and a baby.

In response, I became a workaholic, volunteering for every assignment, just so I didn't have to go home. Eventually, I realized I couldn't hide behind my job. Still, I didn't know what to do.

When we learned that Krista's brother and wife were expecting a child, Krista told me again that she wanted a baby. I asked, "Are you mad? This relationship isn't working. We can't bring a baby into it."

"I'm the oldest," she replied. "I should be the one to have the first grandchild."

Without my consent, Krista became pregnant and gave birth to a beautiful girl. We named the baby Addison. Krista's mother came from Pennsylvania to help. Then, before I knew what was happening, Krista and her mom rented a U-Haul and left. They simply took my 3-day-old baby, along with all my dreams, and left.

CHAPTER 5

MIDFLIGHT CRASH

K RISTA AND HER MOM took my beautiful baby, Addison, to Western Pennsylvania, thousands of miles away from me in Corpus Christi, Texas. With the house empty and quiet, I had plenty of time to try to make sense of my life. I was at my lowest low, and frantic to be involved in my baby's life.

I had tried everything I could think of to save my marriage. Krista had repeatedly told me I was a piece of crap, and it kept me off balance. A counselor had explained to me that Krista habitually did this to make herself feel better. The unfortunate fact was, I believed her. I didn't feel worthy, and I didn't stand up for myself. I can't find the words to express how miserable and confused I was. Professionally, and even personally, I knew that I was gifted, but the gifts I didn't possess were confidence and backbone. This was especially true at home.

My accident had triggered a lingering insecurity. Graduating from flight school had helped with the fear that I had sustained permanent brain damage no one would tell me about, but I still felt that everybody was better than I was, that their ideas were better.

At work, I was more confident. As chairman of the Flight Evaluation Board, I oversaw everyone's qualifications. When it came to doing the right thing on the job, especially when it came to safety violations, I did have a backbone. The rank on my shoulder, however, didn't match this significant responsibility. The result was conflict with commanders. I found myself going head-to-head with senior officers, a dangerous thing to do in the military.

For example, one pilot who was getting a divorce was distracted and making poor decisions. For safety's sake, he needed to lose his wings. When I recommended this, a commander overrode my decision and screamed at me. The pilot in question later crashed an airplane carrying a crew of five.

With my personal life a mess and stressful conflict at work, I was exhausted. A friend heard about my struggles at work and said, "Dave, the Coast Guard doesn't care about you. While you are giving your all, they are simply using you. You need to step away."

My friend's words struck home and knocked me down in yet another way. In response, I went on a two and a half-day bender. While sobering up, I called off sick to give myself time to recover before returning to work.

Meanwhile, Mike, a drinking buddy and colleague from my pilot group, had asked me to give him advice about bulking up. On the day I was recovering from my bender, I met Mike at a health and vitamin store to help him pick out the right products to meet his goal. Afterward, Mike turned me in to the Coast Guard for shirking duty. As a result, I was taken off the schedule.

My operations supervisor, having observed me at work for a long time, finally had a heart-to-heart conversation with me. "Dave, he said, these people are *not* your friends. They pretend to be your friends because of your role as chairman of the Flight Evaluation Board. You have to quit being the victim."

The commander's words, following Krista's deception and Mike's betrayal, hit their mark. I was stunned at the realization that while I was fighting for right and friendship, those around me were busy with their own self-centered agendas.

For all my professional accomplishments, I *was* behaving like a pushover, a pussy. I had no grit for one-on-one situations. I had allowed Krista and her mom to beat me down, and fake friends to abuse me. In my downward spiral, I had been using alcohol as a crutch. Like drugs, excessive eating, and other escape strategies, this was only making things worse. I decided it was time to find my courage and begin to take care of myself physically, mentally, and spiritually. There was no other way to move forward.

This series of experiences marked the beginning of Dave becoming Dave. Because I didn't know who was for me and who was against me, I shut nearly everyone out. I requested a transfer out of the Coast Guard to the National Guard. I wanted to move to Pennsylvania to be near Addison. I had something to fight for, and I was determined to give it my all. No matter how dark the time, I wasn't going to give up on myself or on a relationship with my child.

The Coast Guard didn't want to let me go, and in the end, the secretary of Homeland Security had to sign the paperwork for the transfer. Even with this official signature, the transfer wasn't smooth. I needed top secret clearance for the job with the National Guard, and the process stalled out.

In my 30s, I again found myself moving from the role of chief pilot in the Coast Guard to an hourly worker in the pizza shop where I had worked as a high school and college student. And like a kid, I also lived in my mom's basement—again. It took nearly a year for my clearance to come through. I kept a smile on my face as I served pizza, cleaned toilets, scrubbed floors, and blew through my savings. My job was a step-down in status, but it deserved my 110 percent.

During this time, Krista was saying she wanted us to get back together. I wanted to believe her, but it was clear she'd prefer if I simply disappeared. I kept making the effort to see my daughter.

Once my clearance came through, I was stationed at the 171 Air Refueling Wing in Pittsburgh, PA. I had been working on myself, and by that point, I was fit and trim. The Guard sent me to a three-week training known as SERE (Survive, Evade, Resist, Escape) School. This was an intense experience of discovering what I and 84 others could do in the face of challenges.

To say that SERE training was tough doesn't do it justice. In fact, I lost 20 pounds in the first week and a half. In the end, however, I came away built up, having tested my own strength and resilience. This was a turning point at which I finally began to believe in myself and like myself.

I began even more earnestly seeking self-awareness to find my best self as a person—body, mind, and soul. I was looking for a purpose, some reason bigger than myself and human circumstances to live for. I had always believed I survived the plane crash for a reason, and I was now intent upon finding that reason.

The one thing I never expected was another plane crash, but one was coming, and soon. It happened when I was co-pilot on a refueling exercise.

The pilot, Ray, and I were flying a KC-135 aircraft with the job of off-loading 30,000 pounds of fuel while in midflight to a C-130, a smaller and slower aircraft. Obviously, this is a dangerous task which requires precision, made even more difficult because the C-130 is refueled from behind the plane, where the pilots can't see what is happening.

A boom with a fuel nozzle in the back of the KC-135 connects to the smaller plane and delivers the fuel under the supervision of the boom operator. Once the transfer is complete, the planes separate and the C-130 drops off.

In training, they tell pilots they can determine how serious an emergency separation is by the volume of the boom operator's voice while announcing the breakaway. On this day, things didn't go well at all.

As pilots, we heard a loud shout from the boom operator and knew something was seriously wrong. In fact, the planes had become locked in descent, smashing up the fuel nozzle and nearly taking off the tail of our plane. We had a mid-air fender bender that narrowly missed becoming a fatal accident. The difference between my life and death that day was about five feet.

I remember hearing the shout and having no way to know the nature or severity of the problem. I also had no control over what was happening. There was nothing I could do. Time hung in the air as I asked myself, "Are we crashing? Is this it?" Not knowing what was happening in this situation was one of the worst feelings I've ever had. For the second time, I was facing death by plane crash.

The pilot and I managed to fly back to Pittsburgh and were immediately sent to the hospital where technicians took vial after vial of blood as well as cups of urine. One healthcare worker questioned me, asking, "What's going on? You don't look injured or sick."

I replied, "Well, we crashed a military jet."

The remark was typical of smart-mouth me, but that doesn't mean the incident didn't shake me. Once again, I had an impossible-to-ignore wake-up call to the fragility of life and the need to live my best possible life.

My response to this second shakeup was quite different from my response to the first. I had been clarifying my purpose, building my inner strength and confidence, building my relationship with God, and reaching peace with my own mortality. The difference was huge. Where it had taken me two years from the first crash to get back in a cockpit with confidence, this time it took two weeks. My commitment to becoming the best person I could be was even stronger.

* * * * *

Careerwise, the next logical step seemed to be in the direction of the commercial airlines—the job I'd dreamed of as a child and as a college student. It was time to start submitting applications for that long-awaited job. I had a connection in FedEx who had promised me an interview. I confidently submitted an application, only to find that no interview was forthcoming. When that door was dramatically shut unexpectedly, I knew I was being guided in a different direction.

In 2012, the Air Force deployed me to Qatar to fight the war in Afghanistan. Before leaving the country, I devoted some special time to be with my mom and my dog, Bailey. My mom was (and is) an exemplary parent, and I appreciate how she was always there for me. Knowing my quest to become the best person I could be, she gave me a book by Joel Osteen to take along: *Become a Better You: 7 Keys to Improving Your Life Every Day.*

Bailey, who was near the end of her life, had been with me since just before the accident. Through the dramatic ups and downs of 14 years, Bailey had been my companion, a close and constant friend. Since she would likely die before I returned, I cherished the last bit of time we had.

I was on base doing paperwork after flying a combat sortie in a Stratotanker KC-135, when the email from Mom came: "Bailey left us." Perhaps it was the exhaustion of the ten and a half-hour day of combat that made the loss hit me hard. It was not that the news was a surprise; I had known Bailey wouldn't be there to greet me when I returned home.

Whatever it was, Mom's email about Bailey triggered an anguished night in the desert. I prayed, begging the Universe to let me know the purpose for which I had survived my crash. I was outside at 4 a.m. in 138-degree heat when a passage from Joel Osteen's book came to mind. He had written something to the effect of, "All the wisdom and wealth of the world lies in books not written."

"What do you want me to do?" I asked in frustration. "Write a book?!"

Just then, a fireball of a shooting star raced across the sky. The star was so bright that I thought it was a missile. I ran for the bunker.

Once I realized I had seen a star rather than a missile, I thought, "There is no way that just happened." And then I thought, "Dave Moore doesn't even read books!" I spent the rest of the deployment looking for huge shooting stars, thinking it was a phenomenon of that region. I didn't see even one. I came home and started writing a book.

Marley & Me was popular at the time, so I thought I should write about Bailey and me. But I needed help. When my 11th grade teacher, Mr. Steiner, answered my phone call, he said, "I'm very surprised to be hearing from you. I'm very surprised you are writing a book. Send me a few chapters." I guess Mr. Steiner had noticed that I was playing football when other kids were in his book club.

In response to my chapters, Mr. Steiner said, "The only thing worse than your grammar is your disrespect for a paragraph."

Even so, Mr. Steiner helped.

CHAPTER 6

NEW MARRIAGE, NEW PATH

ACK ON US SOIL, and long after my divorce, I was
stationed at the base outside of Pittsburgh. It was
uncanny how often I ran into a beautiful girl named
Kendal. She was in the reserves, serving a weekend a
month and two weeks per year, while I was working
full-time in the Air National Guard.

As a pilot, I was in operations; Kendal was in the
administrative office. Yet, I kept seeing this girl and
thinking she had good energy. I'd quickly stop myself,
given that I was an officer and she was enlisted; dating
was against the rules. I kept telling myself to get Kendal
out of my mind.

Still badly burned from my marriage to Krista, I had
no interest in even the slightest risk of relationship pain.
I was using my time to work on bettering myself and
learning to love myself. Although I had come a long
way already, I had some distance to go in the area of
self-improvement. In fact, I occasionally still wore a

T-shirt that read, "Beers fear me. Hooter girls love me." The process of improving myself was more like a long journey than a quick race.

My quest to be the best dad I could be to Addison involved continually fighting with Krista's parents, who just wanted me out of the picture. I spent a lot of time at the gym. My goal was to be better than the old self who used alcohol to escape pain.

On a day in January 2013, everyone on base was gathered in the auditorium for a Commander's Call, a day of government-mandated training. As I was standing with the pilots, someone said something about snacks. Ever a smart-mouth, I said, "Hey, Colonel, are we having snacks?"

Pissed off, he answered, "Captain Moore, this isn't kindergarten."

I quipped, "I guess I shouldn't expect a nap."

Seeing his reaction, I quickly veered away from the command group and saw Kendal, beautiful as ever. We started to talk, and before long, we were in the back of the room enjoying a long conversation. A portion of that conversation was about eating and fitness, a favorite topic of Kendal's. In fact, people at the base teased Kendal because she always had a healthy stash of nuts and berries with her, a bit like a squirrel.

At 5'8", I had been struggling to lose weight my whole life. My Italian genes made me thick and stocky, and my Italian mother made sure I loved lasagna and all things carbohydrate. This was a problem, given that keeping my job in the military required me to weigh in at 180 pounds. I'm confident I tried every diet in the book, including South Beach, Atkins, and Paleo, as well as laxatives, all just to keep my job! I knew diets were neither good for my body nor effective, but I didn't know what else to do.

Kendal talked about self-care and how it must include the body, mind, and soul. She shared interesting information about current food research, including that each individual must discover what foods fit his or her body type. Not only was this woman beautiful, she was intelligent and interesting.

At some point in the conversation, Kendal put her number in my phone. When I called, we spoke for an hour. The next time I approached Kendal, I was nervous and made up a lame question about healthcare. She responded, "I don't know anything about healthcare, but I would like to go to dinner."

We went to Jerome Bettis' Grille 36 in Pittsburgh's North Side, and Kendal mistakenly called me Matt. My snap back at her caught the attention of two Steelers sitting at the next table. They found her mistake and my reaction hilarious.

A week later, we got together again. Kendal showed up with a devotional called *Our Daily Bread* and a Bible. We began our relationship by reading and learning together. There was such a natural fit between us that my 140-pound Rottweiler rolled on his back and let

Kendal rub his belly. The big dog was also gentle to Kendal's Maltese-Poodle mix.

Six months later, we were walking the dogs on a country club golf course when I blurted out, "Let's get married." I caught Kendal by surprise, and she said she liked the way things were. The following day, Kendal called and wanted to talk about what "we talked about on the golf course." I quipped, "Do you mean going for a sandwich at Subway?"

Soon after, at sunset on the same golf course, I gave her the formal proposal she deserved—on my knee with a ring to present. After our embrace, Kendal gazed at the ring while I looked up at the sky. Beside the sun, I saw a huge black planet with a ring around it. "Kendal," I said, "Do you see that?!" I kept looking back at that planet for a long time; it remained there. I took it as a validation of the marriage.

Kendal and I were married in October, in celebration of her 27th birthday, nine months after Commander's Call where we had hung out that first time.

At the time, my career was solid, and as an officer, I made good money. Kendal, a country girl, felt great about our relationship and our financial situation. On the other hand, I knew it was time to change careers to continue my growth. I had the ability to contribute much more than I was at the type of assignments given to me. Yet, things were fine, because I was so grateful for my wife—a truly good person—and I was using the time to better myself.

NEW MARRIAGE, NEW PATH   61

With Mr. Steiner's help, I had completed my book. I had also recently met Jeff Tobe, a professional speaker who encouraged me to share my story and inspiration on the stage. After speaking at a few schools, Kendal and I started Moore Motivated and envisioned making a difference in the lives of audience members. I could finally see the purpose in surviving my accident was to help others grow while striving to become the person I was meant to be. If I could change or help one struggling teenager, I'd be right where I needed to be.

During this wonderful time, I had a gut feeling that a change was coming. Sure enough, a major snafu occurred with paperwork for a promotion I was due. As a result, I learned on my birthday in June of 2014 that I was being was being forced out of the military.

The snafu involved paperwork being sent to the wrong email, deadlines being missed as a result, and my being disqualified for promotion twice. As a result of two disqualifications, no matter that I wasn't at fault, I was automatically kicked out of the service.

The Air Force tried to rectify the situation by sending my case to a special review board of Congress. I knew in my gut that it wasn't going to work out, and I told those trying to help me that my discharge was God's will. They thought I was crazy.

Due to a forced government shutdown, the special review board didn't meet, and I was, in fact, out of a job. Kendal and I went from a comfortable lifestyle to living in my mom's basement.

Then, a job flying a Falcon 50 for Channellock, a company that produces hand tools, fell in my lap. With headquarters in Meadville, PA, this company is best known for manufacturing more than 140 types of pliers—particularly its eponymous tongue-and-groove, slip-joint pliers.

The company sent me to Texas for three weeks of training, and a season of exceptional growth began for Kendal and me. While I was in class all day each day, Kendal walked around at the mall, giving out my business cards and trying to sell books—talking to anyone who would listen about Moore Motivated and my inspiring story. You might say the response was less than overwhelming. One Christian bookstore did take the book on consignment. While we were in the store delivering the books, we saw a picture of Jesus that stopped us in our tracks.

We were both so moved by this picture that we bought it and hung it in our hotel room. Hanging there, Jesus seemed to be looking right at us, reminding us that we needed to work more on our very beings. We needed to increase our morality, yes, but the challenge extended much further. We needed to find the best person(s) inside us, individually and as a couple, and lock arms to fulfill our mission. We had to set the bar higher and pursue excellence, leaving any sense of mediocrity permanently behind.

During those three weeks in Texas, our sense of spirituality was heightened in so many ways. I vividly remember Kendal and me talking with an old B-17 tail gunner who was shot down during WWII. He told the story of his airplane breaking in half and catching fire. He was the only survivor. Aware that he should not be alive, the man told us, "Jesus reached in there and pulled me out. No one will listen to me." Having been "pulled out" of a plane crash myself, I still get shivers when I think of that old man.

On the job, I was preparing to take over for the chief pilot, Paul, who was retiring from Channellock. As it turned out, Paul had an ugly personal agenda. After my training, we flew on assignment to Germany, where Paul proceeded to get drunk and tell me I was a piece of shit. The abuse hit hard, and, once again, I felt Krista had been right. I was soft—and it seemed that becoming increasingly moral had made me even softer. I didn't trust my own instincts and decisions. Not knowing what else to do, I kept busy and avoided Paul. That just made him angrier. The work situation became intolerable.

Soon after Paul shared his lousy assessment of me, we took a harrowing flight across the ocean in a snowstorm, during which Paul earned a violation. He and I landed at Hilton Head where, based on Paul's agenda and his relationship with the company CEO, I got fired after only five months with the company.

Looking back, I see my time at Channellock as a lesson in hardening. Throughout this experience, as well as ones that had come before, I was learning to build a thicker skin and necessary grit. I needed to detach myself from the negativity and abuse of others—and to learn to love and believe in myself. To be a leader, I needed to trust my decisions and stand behind them. I needed to learn that I didn't have to allow others to take me down, as I had with Krista. I had other choices. I could choose to step into my own power or give it away. No one could take my power unless I allowed it.

The idea that morality makes you soft is a myth. False niceness, a sense of inferiority, and fake humility make you soft. Leaders of the highest morality and integrity stand up for themselves and their beliefs. In fact, leadership frequently involves taking unpopular stands. Leaders confront wrongs when others turn the other way. They protect those who report to them from injustice. These were my lessons cemented at Channellock, short as my time there was. It was time to move to my next lesson.

Financially down to nothing, Kendal and I again moved to my mom's basement, until we decided we should take our one car and three dogs to Pensacola, which had been a good place for me in the past. Living on a $2,000 loan from my mom, we subsisted on rice cakes in a Red Roof Inn.

Sweetly naïve, Kendal at first thought the woman in the next room simply had a bunch of boyfriends, and the guys on the other side had a lot of visitors. I quickly moved us to another motel, but the options within our budget weren't all that much better.

Despite the accomplishments detailed on my resume, I just couldn't get a job. It was a frustrating and humiliating reality I couldn't understand. While job hunting, I tried to book speaking events, and felt elated when I booked an unpaid luncheon speech at the local Rotary Club. I also became an Uber driver, one of the first in Pensacola. I gave out my business cards for Moore Motivated to all my passengers.

Financially, every day was a struggle. As an Uber driver, I was limited because there was a fee of one dollar to cross the bridge from Pensacola to Pensacola Beach, where tourists wanted to go. Since I didn't have the dollar, I couldn't transport people from the airport to their vacation rentals. Even so, I was as determined to be a 5-star Uber driver as I had been a 5-star pizza employee; I believe in being my best in any job.

I believe all work is honorable and deserves my highest effort—and no matter where any of us happen to be, we have a lot higher to go. I'm committed to leaving every situation better than I found it. For me, this is a leadership philosophy. Every job that helps others is honorable, and every point is simply a starting point. My goal was to become a leader worth following, even behind the wheel of an Uber. I'm not saying I found it easy to give my best to the job every day. Holding myself accountable to my own standards is the hardest part of personal growth.

While I was driving for Uber, Kendal took a job scrubbing dogs. We put all of our effort into growing into our best selves, even as we were exhausted from trying to make ends meet. I remember a time I needed $1,700 to pay our bills, and there happened to be a big event in Orange Beach, Alabama, roughly 30 miles from

Pensacola. I drove Uber passengers for 20 hours and was on top of the world when I made $1,885 in fares. Then I got a bolt impaled in my tire, and all my energy, as well as the few excess dollars, drained away. As always, I was provided just enough for the lesson I needed to learn.

Kendal's willingness to work beside me during this time was amazing. The man she had married was a respectable military officer with a respectable salary. And here she was, not that long after, living in cheap motels and scrubbing her hands raw while this man she had married drove Uber. Kendal smelled so bad at the end of each workday, that I'd ask her to take a shower the minute she walked in the door.

Yet, Kendal didn't call me a loser or any other derogatory term. The contrast between my marriage to Kendal and my marriage to Krista couldn't be sharper. Kendal has believed in me from the start and has always been my partner in the quest to serve a purpose bigger than ourselves. Kendal was the one sitting beside me when we created the vision for Moore Motivated. I'm so grateful to have a wife who loves me for who I am rather than any lifestyle I can provide. Together, we believe we can make the world a better place. She plays a vital role in all we do.

Our struggle in Pensacola went on for months, until three great job opportunities came my way at the same time. While it didn't make a lot of sense to me, I knew in my heart I was to accept the offer to work in sales for National Equipment Service (NES), an organization that rents construction equipment—something I knew nothing about.

I didn't know why I should take this job; I just knew I should. I didn't even have a starting point in the industry, but I was willing to throw myself in. It turned out that the job was my opportunity to be raised up in sales.

I took over the established territory of a top general manager who mentored me in the business. I soaked up the opportunity to learn and gave 110 percent effort. I ended up being top salesperson at the company. I learned the fundamentals and finesse used by successful salespeople, skills that would pave the way to prosperity again and again.

CHAPTER 7

STRUGGLES AND LEGAL FEES

WHILE I WAS THRIVING in my role as #1 sales representative for National Equipment Sales (NES), Kendal was running Moore Motivated from our home in Pensacola. She was passionate about spreading our lessons about being a leader worthy of being followed. She was also pregnant with our first child, Favianna. We were riding on a cloud.

I remember the heady feeling of our first full-fee event. I was spot-on in every sense as I spoke before an audience in California. They demonstrated their enthusiasm with applause and by requesting selfies with me. I felt that Kendal and I had made it—our dream of changing lives with my story on stage was realized. Our purpose was being fulfilled.

Well, maybe we weren't there just yet. Soon after this great experience, Kendal booked a presentation for me in Mobil, Alabama. Failing to take the assignment seriously, I showed up unprepared.

I thought I would be speaking to doctors and was pumped to share my inspiring thoughts with them. I expected to use my energy and spontaneity to charm the audience as I had in California. I had visions of applause and more selfies.

It turned out that the audience was made up of mentally handicapped children. Virtually nothing I had to say was spot-on. I stumbled and stuttered and failed. This disaster was one of the most humbling experiences of my life. Doctors and dignitaries were in the room; they simply weren't the people I was meant to address. I wanted to run out of the room and hide.

In my hotel room after the presentation, I knew one thing for sure: I never wanted to feel that way again. As I lay in bed, I saw, through a crack in the draperies, a big church steeple. I realized that having what I believed to be a spiritual calling did not entitle me to be lazy. Raw talent, ego, and flying by the seat of one's pants are not welcome or effective ingredients when it comes to serving others.

My journey to success was not going to be a straight and easy line. I had relied on talent and charisma throughout my life, and now it was not enough. If I wanted to succeed as a professional speaker, I would have to slow down and perform my due diligence. I would have to research the needs of each audience and give them my absolute best. I needed to give 110 percent every time, just as I did in the pizza shop. Whatever had given me the idea that I could do less? It was, once again, time to wake up.

Meanwhile, things were going wonderfully at NES. I was getting more and more customers and accounts. And now that Kendal and I could afford to eat more than rice cakes, her commitment to healthy living could flourish. I was blessed with a fabulous resource and partner in my goal of becoming strong in body, mind, and spirit.

By this time, I had made some progress in my journey toward understanding what it takes to be physically fit, but I still had a lot to learn. At one point during my quest to keep my weight down for my job at the Guard, I had gotten into a conversation with Phil, a fellow pilot and officer. I was feeling good about myself because I was regularly doing the Insanity Workout, an intense total body workout that uses your own body weight for resistance. The program is based on a fitness method called "max interval training." Proponents claim that exercising at this extreme intensity level will help you burn up to 1,000 calories an hour.

This season of practicing the Intensity Workout was one of the "lean" times in my lifelong fluctuation between lean and fat. Phil, however, was even leaner. He had lost 37 pounds through intermittent fasting. In talking to him, I learned that there are different types of intermittent fasting. Phil was practicing the type that calls for restricting food intake to certain hours each day. Phil's daily window was from 11 to 7.

I protested, "That practice can't be right. Breakfast is the most important meal of the day! Experts have been telling us that forever."

Phil shook his head and replied, "Dave, look at me. I just lost 37 pounds, and I feel great." I couldn't deny the results, so I gave intermittent fasting a try and experienced immediate results. Research indicates that this approach to eating, which is not a diet, makes sense because it mirrors the eating pattern of our ancestors.

As hunter/gatherers, our ancestors didn't graze all day. While in terms of evolution, we are not that far from these ancestors, we've altered the human perspective on eating drastically. At least in the developed world, we've made eating a social practice rather than a means of survival.

I was having great success with my eating window, but that didn't mean that I was eating the healthiest foods. Kendal taught me that a human being is an organism that needs intentional care to thrive. She helped me understand how sugar and processed foods hurt us. Now that we had the means to do so, we invested in eating clean food, including organic produce and grass-fed beef. We ate well and worked out. We were both becoming stronger in every sense.

But Krista and her parents were still behaving spitefully, trying to keep me from seeing Addison. Kendal and I would drive all night from Florida to Pennsylvania, and then Krista wouldn't let me see my daughter. My professional life and family life with Kendal were finally going smoothly, and I was gaining confidence as a person. Yet, I was stuck in a constant fight with Krista.

Krista invented reasons to block my visits, such as fevers and other devised obstacles. I was afraid of losing my child and determined not to let it happen. Kendal and I undertook what we referred to as "Operation Addi."

Meanwhile, Krista got involved with another man, John, who wanted to be Addi's dad. My initial reaction was to feel sorry for John, believing that Krista would just use him as she had used me. But John didn't make it easy for me to hold onto that perspective.

One day, we attended the open house at Addi's school. When we arrived, I said to Krista and John, "We can do this in one of two ways—"

John interrupted to say, "I'll be calling the shots here!"

Just as quickly, I responded, "No, you will not!" Heated words flew back and forth.

Krista filed an emergency custody hearing, charging me with being verbally abusive to her at the school's open house. Trying to manage the conflict from a distance became too much, and I resigned from NES. They offered me a transfer, but I chose not to take it. Kendal and I decided to step out and build Moore Motivated. From a financial perspective, the decision was a big mistake, and we burned through our saving quickly.

The custody case was moved to the county where Krista's wealthy parents knew all the judges and had plenty of money to throw at the legal battle that ensued. They were engaged in country club politics, while I had no money and no job, just the looming threat that they would take my child away.

Once again, I couldn't get a job during a recession—at least not one that made sense geographically. I could sell avionics in Florida or Texas, but such jobs didn't exist in Pennsylvania. I turned the jobs down and borrowed $5,000 from my mom to pay legal fees. To say this was a difficult time is an understatement. Thankfully, my faith in God sustained me. I knew it would all be okay.

In the end, the judge ordered the arrangement I had been asking for all along: Addi would be with us every other weekend, alternating holidays, and half of the summer. I had known it was a reasonable request, and I hadn't wanted to go to court. The whole process seemed like it would be a waste of time and money, causing stress for Addi—who was seven at the time—and everyone else too. But, with the judge's decision, a weight I had been carrying for years was lifted. I felt free, like a brand-new person.

I took a job with Emerald Equipment Company selling million-dollar machines that crushed rocks. I remember the first time these magnificent machines were demonstrated for me; they left me covered in dust. My heart sank, but I needed the job. Because my heart wasn't in it, I couldn't rise to my best results, but I could still give 110 percent. I got big accounts for the company, adhering to a commitment to leave every job better than I found it.

We had enough money again, and I had a relationship with Addi. Favianna had been born in September of 2016 and was a wonderful child. Kendal and I welcomed another daughter, Olivia, in 2017, when Favianna was 13 months old.

Our time in Pennsylvania was one of healing. The conflict and trial were repercussions from what I had allowed to happen in my marriage with Krista. Getting successfully through that helped me close a door to the nagging feelings of guilt and fear I had carried with me from that time.

I was doing well in my job, but I wasn't flourishing because my heart wasn't in equipment sales. I also couldn't seem to get any traction around my identity as an inspirational speaker on leadership in my hometown. There is a safety net with people that have known you your whole life; it's difficult to break out of patterns and the limited expectations others have for you.

We decided to move to Warren, Ohio, when Olivia was a year old and Favianna was two. I was still working at Emerald Equipment, but I soon found myself looking for a next step, for my lane where I could make a tangible contribution.

Moore Motivated had been growing since the move, and the theme of becoming a leader worth following took roots. Kendal continued to run the business and book presentations for me. For my part, I was showing up as I should—enthusiastically, well-prepared, and with my ego in check. Feedback was great, and Kendal and I were both thrilled with the difference my story was making in others' lives.

In the preface to this book, I described my life as a roller coaster of triumphs, setbacks, and self-imposed obstacles. In fitness, finances, and relationships, I've been all over the place. I'm in a great place now, but I'm guessing that bumps—big and small—will be a part of my future.

I've discovered that the path to success isn't a straight line for anyone. Countless stories of successful entrepreneurs and influential leaders include times of failure, bankruptcy, and/or crushing defeat. True winners climb and fall as many times as needed and give their absolute best in what they are doing in the here and now. We all need to grow at our own pace, trust the process, and stop worrying about what other people do or think. Whether you are at the top or the bottom of the roller coaster, you are still on the ride, and that is what really counts.

CHAPTER 8

MARCHING ORDERS

W HEN I SAW AN AD for Jet It, LLC, a start-up company based on fractional ownership of the HondaJet, I got tingles down my spine and immediately applied. Now that I was free from the geographical restrictions of court, Krista, and her parents, I could take off professionally.

After reading my resume, the CEO, Glenn Gonzales, set up an interview and hired me on the spot. I was ecstatic! Finally, I was back in the world of aviation, where my passion lay. I had already proven my skills in sales, and, with my heart in this venture, I knew the sky was the limit. The day after I accepted the offer, my territory at Emerald was closed unexpectedly.

In January of 2019, Jet It sent me to get my type rating (agency certification) to fly the HondaJet, and I began flying demos for prospects, all of whom were high net-worth individuals. Within three months, I was vice president of sales for the Northeast. Each morning, I put on a suit and tie and met with prospects and clients. In the process, I met a lot of smart people and took the opportunity to learn from them.

I noticed that many successful people strike a balance between humility and confidence. They know their strengths, and while not thinking of themselves as better than others, they don't let people push them around. One of the themes in my journey to improvement has been the need to toughen up in the right ways. This was reinforced in many of my Jet It encounters.

An example of this continuing need came in a recent encounter with another professional speaker. Because so much of my presentation content stems from my experience as a pilot, I've always worn a flight suit on stage. It takes the guesswork out of what to wear, and I'm comfortable in a flight suit. It feels like a pair of pajamas to me.

The other presenter informed me that he had a trademark for wearing a flight suit on stage, and I needed to stop wearing mine. My first inclination was to simply accept this and back off. When I asked one of my mentors—also a successful speaker—for advice, he reminded me that leaders show up strong, especially in the face of a bully such as this. I kept reminding myself that my goal of being a strong moral person does not mean letting others walk over me. I still wear a flight suit on stage, although it's a different suit than the other speaker's.

Meanwhile, on a demo flight for Jet It, I met Dr. Garo Armen, founder and CEO of Agenus. An overnight trip from New York to Chicago allowed us plenty of time to talk, and I found myself fascinated by what Garo and his company do.

Agenus Inc. is a biotechnology company focused on controlling or curing cancer via immunotherapy. In other words, Agenus seeks to treat cancer with the body's own defenses rather than through chemotherapy. Early products have produced unprecedented clinical benefits for patients, without the side effects of chemo. *Science* magazine hailed cancer immunotherapy as its 2013 Breakthrough of the Year.

Garo, the son of a mechanic, lost his mother to breast cancer and is dedicated to his work of fighting cancer. He is incredibly knowledgeable about how the human body works. Over drinks in Chicago, I shared some of the things that Kendal and I were doing regarding nutrition and health, and Garo shared some of his advanced knowledge with me. We also talked about Moore Motivated and how committed I was to helping people learn how to be a leader worth following. I was thrilled to be having this conversation with such a brilliant man.

As I flew the two of us back to New York the following day, Garo said, "I feel in my gut that we should be working together." We agreed to explore a professional relationship.

Soon after, I went on to make the largest sale ever for Jet It. The time from the customer's demo to closing the sale took one short week. My fellow team members made a big deal of this and started calling me "The Giant Slayer."

While I love to celebrate a victory, I don't think of myself as special. When it comes to sales, I had the best possible opportunity to learn how to succeed from a 30-year veteran at NES. I learned and applied the process, and it worked. In any case, the sale was a huge win for Jet It at a time they needed it. And I could now leave the company after about a year, knowing I had made a real contribution.

I left Jet It and now find that my journey has brought me to an amazing place. Garo hired me as the company's Employee Engagement Specialist, reporting directly to him. It's my job to ensure the company's brilliant scientists and employees stay engaged and motivated. This is a huge shift from sales for me, yet it's a good fit. I'm uniquely qualified by my personal passion and the work I've done over the years learning what it means to be a leader worth following.

At the same time, Garo knows my purpose in Moore Motivated and is 100 percent behind it. He has taught me his system to support the body's health by sustaining an ideal body weight and a strong immune system. I'd been practicing what I learned about intermittent fasting for quite some time. That meant I ate only during an eight-hour window each day. Garo helped me understand why I needed to shorten that window to a single meal each day.

To understand why this is a smart practice, Garo urged me to look to animals in the wild. The cow grazes all day long, but it is not the animal you want on your side in a battle. The lion, who is the embodiment of strength and power, eats one meal a day. Our ancestors, as hunters and gatherers, didn't eat all day either, and the bodies we inhabit evolved from them. From an evolutionary standpoint, our culture rapidly shifted the practice of eating from being a survival necessity to a social event. In many ways, this is killing us.

By eating one meal a day and hydrating throughout, I am not starving my body; I'm allowing it to detox. Research shows that this practice reduces risks for cardiac problems, cancer, obesity, and more. I can testify that it keeps my weight down while increasing my energy and productivity. I've never felt better.

Knowing that my body is functioning at its best not only gives me satisfaction, it also allows me to give my best to my mission in life. I'm not necessarily pushing the pattern that works for me on you. Your body is unique, and I encourage you to discover what works best for you. I do know that grazing all day, especially on processed foods and refined sugars, is toxic to every human body. Do the research and figure out what is best for your body. Make the effort and reap the rewards.

My personal and professional journey is far from over. In October of 2019, Kendal and I welcomed another daughter, Julia Leigh. My work at Agenus is contributing to cutting-edge research and products that save lives in new and exciting ways. My speaking engagements with Moore Motivated are growing in number and impact. Who knows what comes next?

While every day brings surprises and growth, it's time to bring this book to a close. Before I do, I want to tell you about a recent incident that involves yet another plane crash.

I was bringing the HondaJet in for a landing in Nashville on a beautiful day, sunny and dry, with no wind. Nashville was at the end of a six-week drought. It would rain hard the next evening.

After touching down centerline of the runway with one and a half miles of beautifully manicured runway ahead of me to roll to a stop, I was thinking of getting a cup of coffee and refueling once I dropped off the brilliant scientist who was sitting up front with me.

As I came onto the brakes, the plane veered abruptly to the left. I released the brakes, coming back to neutral, thinking a brake had stuck, but when I came back on the brakes, no braking was available. I didn't know it then, but this was due to a braking problem with the original HondaJet, which has since been remade correctly.

I made a split-second decision to ride the jet at 120 feet per second off the runway rather than try to use the nose wheel steering to straighten us out. The plane was at such an angle that I feared a steering maneuver would force a wing, full of fuel, into the runway.

We crossed over to dry, rock-hard grass, and I was able to regain control of the plane and bring us to a stop parallel to the runway. A mere fifteen more yards off the runway and we would have landed in a four-foot ditch and maybe died.

Stunned, I sat in the cockpit and began to yell at the scientist next to me. I accused her of jamming the peddle to the floor, at a loss for anything else that might have pulled us off the runway.

Police trucks and huge firetrucks converged on our little HondaJet next to the runway, and I jumped out to meet the first responders.

"I always thought there would be a third one." I exclaimed to the confused group.

"Anybody hurt?" asked a police officer.

"Just my pride," I responded.

I explained why I had decided to go off the runway.

The head police officer asked me to show him where we had gone off the runway because he couldn't find the tracks. I didn't know. The time from the moment I made my decision until I regained control on the dry, hard ground was a blur. At that point, I still thought the accident was my fault, and that the scientist had gotten excited and stomped the rudder pedal.

When the officer and I finally noticed tracks, we realized they were from the police truck. The truck was making distinct tracks through the grass, but our jet, weighing 2.5 to 3 times the truck, had left no tracks. What's more, the plane hadn't hit even one runway edge light. We had departed the runway at a high velocity, with three landing gears underneath the plane, and we missed every runway edge light. How could that be?

Without the evidence of some grass in the right brake, the FAA inspector declared they would never have known the plane left the runway. The accident was deemed not to be my fault; it was a mechanical problem. The steering was actuating the plane to the left, something HondaJet was able to fix after the crash.

A few days later, I drove a rental car to Washington, DC, where I had a speaking engagement. I was confident I had a killer presentation. Unfortunately, I wasn't ready to give it.

In front of a large audience, speaking about overcoming obstacles, I told the story of this recent crash as an opener. As I told the story in front of the crowd, the reality of what had just happened sunk in. I envisioned the hard ground, the runway edge lights, the four-foot ditch where we could have landed and died. I understood that a decision to try to stay on the runway rather than roll off could have brought death to my passenger and me.

There I was, alive, just days later, telling the story. As the seriousness and mystery of it all settled in, I was overcome. I almost set down the microphone and walked out of the room. I never had wanted to walk out of anywhere so badly in my life. I had a lot of thinking to do.

Somehow, I made it through the speech, but I didn't dazzle my audience, and I didn't teach them much about overcoming obstacles—unless they learned from the grit

I displayed just by showing up. I hated disappointing that audience, and it made me question my goals for Moore Motivated.

A few weeks later, I flew the repaired HondaJet into an airport in Beaver County, a small community in Pennsylvania. My Uber driver, Frisco, showed up at the airport, and excitedly asked, "Are you a pilot?"

I said I was. The driver, from Central America, explained that he had saved $10,000 and wanted to pursue his dream of becoming a pilot. He didn't know how to get started.

I told him about the excellent program the Beaver County Community College offers. It's the program, in fact, that gave me my start.

Little did Frisco know that I was struggling with thoughts of my own future, even during our conversation. I know I can be successful at everything I do. So many easy-to-open doors are sitting in front of me, yet I have this speaking business that had just taken a hard hit. A career in speaking is by far the hardest path to take—

Frisco interrupted my thoughts to say, "Look over there; it's a fox." As he slowed the car to get a good look, he exclaimed, "That's a wolf! Do you see this? That's a wolf.

"I see," I answered.

Frisco was having a harder time digesting the wolf sighting than I was. He said, "I'm getting goose bumps just seeing this!"

I said, "If you had seen all the things I have, you would not be as surprised." I explained that I felt the wolf was a message to me from the Universe, and that I needed to do an Internet search to see what it meant.

After all, I have been around the Beaver County area a lot in my life. I know that wild wolves walking down the road are not a normal sight. In fact, wolves don't even live in the area.

When I googled "wolf" right then, I read that wolves symbolize self-discovery, strength, and courage. I knew immediately what my direction needed to be. I would look past the easy, lucrative opportunities at my door and take the road less traveled.

I got to the place I am today by taking the road less traveled. While for many, I am a lot to digest, I have a lot to offer those who want to become leaders, beginning with how to lead themselves and learn to lead in professional and personal roles.

I encourage you to wake up and take your life off autopilot. You may not be living through plane crashes or seeing wolves walking the streets, but you are living your own challenges. Will you play harder, determined to identify your purpose in life? Will you play to impact your company, family, or world in a way that leaves a legacy? Will you face your own mortality, living so that when your last breath comes you will be satisfied that you have fulfilled your purpose and left the world a better place?

ABOUT THE AUTHOR

GROWING UP, all Dave Moore wanted to do was become a professional pilot. He submerged himself in everything aviation, even qualifying as a flight instructor before finishing college. At 23, he experienced a plane crash that nearly took his life. The result was a crippling fear of flying and a determination to become the best person he could be. Dave wanted to be sure that when he would face death again, he would be proud of the person he had become.

Dave overcame his fear of flying and achieved great things, in both military and civilian life. He earned Navy and Air Force wings, officer status in the Coast Guard and Air Force, and held high-level leadership positions with large teams with large budgets. Dave was Chief Pilot on the HU-25 Falcon Jet in search and rescue missions and flew 39 combat missions in the Middle East. He has held top corporate pilot positions and has been in the top tier of earners in several companies.

Dave is a clearly a winner, but nothing about getting there was easy. The pivot point came when Dave's wife and mother-in-law moved his newborn infant thousands of miles away. Dave decided it was time to wake up and fight for his child. He also decided to become the best version of himself as a father as well as a person who fulfills his life purpose.

Dave's journey to success is a roller coaster of triumphs, setbacks, and self-imposed obstacles. He has been battered, divorced, unemployed, underemployed, unappreciated, and bankrupt. Against all odds, he survived two more plane crashes, remarried, and fathered three more beautiful children.

Now, as founder of Moore Motivated and an international speaker, Dave's mission is to share the lessons he has learned in his tumultuous journey. The story isn't all pretty, but it inspires while it reveals a path to waking up and becoming a winner.

To discover more about Dave:
    www.MooreMotivated.com

FOLLOW DAVE ON SOCIAL MEDIA

LinkedIn
https://www.linkedin.com/in/david-moore-3991192a/

Instagram
https://www.instagram.com/Moore_Motivation/

Facebook
https://www.facebook.com/MooreMotivated/

Twitter
https://twitter.com/DMooreMotivated

YOUR NEXT STEP

I F YOU'VE FOUND THIS BOOK INSPIRATIONAL and would like to find out more about developing yourself personally and professionally, visit MooreMotivated.com. While you are there, order Dave's self-development series, which focuses on personal growth. The materials will take you well outside the box to reach for your best.

Why not bring Dave to your next conference for a keynote tailored just for your organization? You might consider a customized version of one of the following:

- ✈ Wake Up and Win: Taking Your Life Off Autopilot

- ✈ Become a Leader Worth Following

- ✈ Become a Team Member Who Performs Above the Cut

- ✈ Create a Culture that Excites People About Coming to Work

To book Dave:
- ✈ Contact: Kendal@MooreMotivated.com